The Parts of a Book

by Martha E. H. Rustad

Consulting Editor: Gail Saunders-Smith, PhD

Consultant: JoAnne DeLurey Reed, Librarian and Teacher
Scroggins Elementary School, Houston, Texas

CAPSTONE PRESS
a capstone imprint

Pebble Plus Books are published by Capstone Press,
1710 Roe Crest Drive, North Mankato, Minnesota 56003.
www.capstonepub.com

Library of Congress Cataloging-in-Publication Data
Rustad, Martha E. H. (Martha Elizabeth Hillman), 1975–
 The parts of a book / by Martha E. H. Rustad.
  pages cm.—(Pebble plus. Wonderful world of reading)
 Includes bibliographical references and index.
 ISBN 978-1-62065-094-3 (library binding)
 ISBN 978-1-4765-1741-4 (eBook PDF)
1. Books—Juvenile literature. I. Title.
Z116.A2R875 2013
002—dc23
2012030349

Editorial Credits
Erika L. Shores, editor; Veronica Scott, designer; Marcie Spence, media researcher; Laura Manthe, production specialist

Photo Credits
All photos Capstone Studio/Karon Dubke, except Shutterstock: Lichtmeister, cover (books)

Note to Parents and Teachers

The Wonderful World of Reading series supports Common Core State Standards for Language Arts related to craft and structure, to text types and writing purpose, and to research for building and presenting knowledge. This book describes and illustrates the parts of a book. The images support early readers in understanding the text. The repetition of words and phrases helps early readers learn new words. This book also introduces early readers to subject-specific vocabulary words, which are defined in the Glossary section. Early readers may need assistance to read some words and to use the Table of Contents, Glossary, Read More, Internet Sites, and Index sections of the book.

Printed in the United States of America in North Mankato, Minnesota.
092012   006933CGS13

TABLE OF CONTENTS

A Little Trip

Let's go on a trip.

A trip around a book!

Will you choose a print book?

An electronic book, also called

an e-book, is just fine too!

Outside a Book

Our first stop is a print book's
outside edge. It's called the spine.
Hidden stitches hold pages together.
Now tilt your head to read
the title and author.

Next up is the front cover.

There's the title. A picture gives

a big clue about what's inside.

Find the name of the author.

Flip over a print book.

Words tell about the book.

A bar code sits in the corner.

bar code

Inside a Book

Time to go inside the book!

The title page shows the title,

author, and publisher.

On the copyright page, it says

not to copy the book.

copyright page

13

Look at the table of contents.

It's like a map of the book.

Read the chapter names

and find out where to go.

Contents

Next you're at the main text.

It makes up the middle of the book.

Facts fill up nonfiction books.

Stories pack into fiction books.

Back Matter

Where the main text ends,

the back matter begins.

A glossary defines certain words.

Last is the index. It lists topics

and where to find them.

An e-book might have more
to find. Click a picture to hear
a sound. Tap an index word
to jump to the page where it is.

Now we're at THE END.
Are you ready for a trip
around another book?

Glossary

author—a person who writes books

bar code—a band of thick and thin lines printed on books and other items sold in stores; bar codes are read by computers to give the price and other information

copyright—the legal right to a book or other work of art

electronic—powered by electricity

fiction—books that tell stories that are not true

glossary—a list of words and what they mean

index—a list of topics in a book and their locations in a book

nonfiction—books that tell facts that are true

publisher—a company that prints a book

spine—the outside edge of a book

stitch—a loop of string that holds something together

text—the words in a book

Read More

Donovan, Sandy. *Karl and Carolina Uncover the Parts of a Book.* In the Library. Minneapolis: Picture Window Books, 2010.

Rissman, Rebecca. *We All Read.* Disabilities and Differences. Chicago: Heinemann Library, 2009.

Walton, Ruth. *Let's Read a Book.* Let's Find Out. Mankato, Minn.: Sea-to-Sea Publications, 2013.

Internet Sites

FactHound offers a safe, fun way to find Internet sites related to this book. All of the sites on FactHound have been researched by our staff.

Here's all you do:

Visit *www.facthound.com*

Type in this code: 9781620650943

Super-cool stuff! Check out projects, games and lots more at www.capstonekids.com

Index

Word Count: 235
Grade: 1
Early-Intervention Level: 22